ILLUSIONS

An Ode to Life

Dr. Boban Ramesan

Published by Cogitabund LLP

publishing@cogitabund.com
www.cogitabund.com

Illusions: An ode to life

A Cogitabund Book/ published by arrangement with the author

ISBN: 978-93-49383-86-9

Typeset and Cover Design by Cogitabund LLP

Contents

ILLUSIONS

An Ode to Life

Dr. Boban Ramesan

Serenade

The tree gives one shade.
which he believes would never fade,
Little does he know it, too, would go
as the blazing sun goes low,
Or even if he were aware
to recognise that he wouldn't dare,
For it's emblematic of his hopes
a bulwark against the reality of loss,
That the tree would live on forever
as the omniscient parent, the provider,
Whom he cannot simply let die
lest his life would be a painful lie…
The shade is just another shadow.
like the one that would faithfully follow
The man pacing around his cave
till his peaceful rest in the grave…
Nature's bequest to mankind
is the tree with the human mind,
not sprung from the seed on earth
but of a quintessentially divine birth!
The tall tree of unwavering hope
that has the sun nestled at its top,
and is the harbour of the moonlit night
from where the owl takes its flight,
In the earthly garden, the tree of immortality
is silently vocal about the innate frailty

of being human, fearful of death,
unwilling to surrender, even at the last breath …

Bliss in the abyss

An "empty" vessel
elated by the sight of
the raving empty vessels,
who with loudness and pride
applaud the sheer emptiness
of their demigod!
The tyrant is inhuman.
But he's not foolish.
He's a masterful trickster.
who thrives on gullibility,
He is simply a mirror.
of the vileness of the crowd
reflecting their own silliness,
their own fallacy
is what maketh the king!
He's the shrewd tyrant.
who pretends to be a jester,
as the appeasement
is what secures his throne!
There would be no royal.
without the faithful royals,
He knows that well
and locks them in hell
of ignorance and hatred,
The prisoners in Plato's cave
walk around in the modern world

believing they're free
unable to see the chains
to which they're bound
as their king laughs (aloud)
pulling the leashes
to gently entice them
to walk on four legs
not to be human anymore
but most obedient animals!

The circuit

The circuit is closed,
The lid is firm
The jar is airtight,
with no room for freedom,
But the fly still clasps.
on to the vine
of an angel's dream
to fill the skies
with its wings of beauty
and unbridled passions!
Suffocating in real
titillating in surreal,
The jar is still a world.
Though empty and bland
It is a garden pot
with the bed of dreams,
for the aspiring bud;
The roses weren't planted.
They grew from within.
the confines of the jar,
The roots run deep
into the glass table
beginning an unending course
into the heart of the earth…
The circuit opens there.
releasing the hidden seeds

of thoughts and concerns,
inaccessible and illegible
to the goblins of the netherworld!
The lone jar of glass
is buried in the quick sands
of time, with its prisoner,
The dreams don't die.
The fly has fire in its eyes.
to build the castle of hopes
and to conquer its own fear…

"X"

The magical ray, that
Seismically changed the world.
exposing with brutal honesty
the mean unglamorous skeletons
within the allure of fleshy bodies
was in fact a case of mistaken identity,
The birth of a new chapter, it was
In the history of humanity,
but through pure accident!
The genius in Roentgen had discovered.
the key to unlock the phantoms
within the mysterious body
through a beam of light…
Faith was nothing but a balm
a compound of myths and superstitions
to soothe the human sorrows,
a gilded gateway paved with hopes
leading to a path of redemption,
In the dark, gloomy days of old
when every life was as fragile as it was
got deposited in the realm of the unknown;
Life was a planetary journey in hell.
over which man had no say whatsoever,
regulated by the forces draped in clouds!
No elaboration of ancient rituals
or bearing the extreme pain of penitences

could heal the callous consumption
that ravaged the populations,
devouring lives without any mercy
as the gods watched in vain
from the galleries above,
in flamboyant picture frames
blinded and deafened by human ignorance!
It was not the "miasma."
But an army of invisibles, the microbes
that no man was aware of,
as his intellect wasn't fully awake
to evolve with the changing times;
The unknown ray, the "X"-ray
shed light on the bodily interiors
unpretentious yet intricate
to be studied with precision
for securing the health of posterity;
A fathomless treasure of such "X-s."
exist in the alcoves of the universe,
for the restless mind to dream about
to strive the hardest
to chisel out the truth
from the rocky stones of myths!

Being

If only the flower
could gesticulate
or put it in words
as the sight entices
with its fragrance,
as if the petals
the delicate artworks
are cherubic wings
of an ethereal being
happening to be here
in a forsaken world,
If only the being
within the floral drapery
could wake up the man
Who is lost in the beauty?
of the stunning display,
that it is nothing but a chapter
of an intricate illusion,
a poignant reminder
of the frivolity of a dream,
The banality of forgetfulness
the hallmark of being human…
If only man could be awakened
to the reality of impermanence,
the transitory thrills
that enliven the journey

would've made more sense,
as not just a sight to savour
But as a unique experience
of flowing along with nature
as a moment to be cherished,
If he had the candour
to submit to that sublimity
of a sense of being,
belonging to the tilled soil
as the soul of the earth,
as a flower in the garden
of universal humanity
with the fragrance of goodness,
He wouldn't have sought in vain.
any heavens for spiritual gain
Or be rabidly delusional about a hell
If his mind was healthy and well …

Between gods and rocks

The god of fire
finds his relevance
In the god of the winds,
One doesn't exist
without the other!
The primeval forces
come to light
from behind the ornate masks
as reason shines high;
The moon is poetic
despite being a desolate rock,
the mother pond
pregnant with her ecosystem
thrives in the thoughts
of the delightful moonlight,
knowing well that it's an illusion
of the reflected light;
The stars are tantalising.
though they've long been dead,
the mirage of the skies
It is dynamic in its stillness.
The mind imagines
Its journey into eternity
though the bodily life
is fixed within the finitude,
the half-burnt candle

hopes for a rejuvenation
in the crystal case of youthfulness;
Between the many gods
and the cold rocks in the skies
stands transfixed, the man
with his prayerful lips
rhythmically uttering words
borne out of his mind
to prove his piety to himself…
As life seems unreal
In a world where death is certain,
He splits his sphere of thoughts.
into two: one for this world
and another for the netherworld,
Unable to disentangle himself
from the dense fog of confusion
He loses out in both lives,
Devoid of the freedom of thought
and never realising his soul,
He ends up being just another beetle.
that doesn't want to know
the impassive shadows of death
lurking in the benign anthill…

The cat's dinner

The cat didn't roar,
It was like lightning.
swift as nature desired,
one pounce,a huge maul
and with a kiss on the carotid
It all went eerily silent…
The body was dead
juice exuded from the meat
like bleeding tomatoes;
The tables suddenly turned,
the celebration of human life
becoming a welcome feast
for the pregnant lioness
Who lanced the warm flesh?
with cold meditative eyes;
The beast has no taste
for esoteric philosophy,
She is wedded to her "gut "instincts,
The unwritten law of the jungle
That calls for opportunistic kill!
The beauty of the wild,
The lioness with her shiny coat
has the prime aesthetic sense
to behold the meat
and secure the feed of the day
be it from a human, or

some other hapless animal
with enough stacks of protein
to satiate her appetite!
She wouldn't shed tears
as a sign of solidarity
with human grief or loss,
It was the error of the human.
to judge her as docile
and nonviolent from a distance,
There is no good or evil.
in the family of the big cats,
Aliens are human concepts.
of malevolence or violence,
The kill is to slake the appetite.
and sink into a snoring slumber,
She knows not the pleasure.
of bloody vengeance,
Nor has she any intention
for coronation on the throne of blood!
The cat has no madness of fame.
Nor does she covet any power,
She honestly brandished her canines.
musty yellow and evidently merciless,
She, being a beast, smelt of death.
Her calmness wasn't a masquerade.
but an elegance, a natural charm;
Yet, the man being human
was drawn into the illusion
of being Daniel in the lions' den,
Merciful indeed must be the gods.
Who saved the man on time!

The man romanced the image.
of the pregnant lioness,
as an object of ethereal beauty
with lyrics in her every move,
like the Rubensian painting!
He would come to adore
the mellowed giant of a cat
shying away from the blazing sun
under the shade of the tree,
The chords were pulled at heart.
as if the beast were a woman
of the same species he belonged to!
What the man wished long to see
He would endow the animal,
eternally beauteous as in poetry
An allegory to an extinct goddess!
The lioness was helpless.
as she knew not the human fantasies
or her idolisation on the high pedestal,
As the man threw the windows open
rejoicing at the rendezvous with her,
She was reluctant at first.
as it is the ingrained nature of her being,
But the stranger appeared delighted.
to offer her all the flesh of his body
The wild cat is an honest animal.
who truthfully follows her own instincts
She made a jump at him for the meat,
And man, being a curiously complex animal.
Who couldn't tell imagination from reality?
was steeped in the stupor of stupidity

even when the teeth dug in deep
and pain seared through his neck…
The lioness calmly walked away.
with a massive chunk of flesh
torn from the dreamy-eyed man,
He no longer knew any pain.
As silence reigned and the forest slept
The giant paws retreated to the den.
deep in the heart of the wilderness,
Whilst the cold, moist eyes gazed vacantly
at the track that beauty had trodden…

Whereto?

Wherefrom is the smoke?
misting the crimson dusk
ushering in a wintry feeling
In the heart of spring?
It's the bonfire of love.
fuelled by the longings,
the flames devouring
the last rib of the skeleton
of souls that've been torn apart
by the fists of fate...
The pyre of concealed hopes
and vacated dreams
reduced to a burning wick,
a minuscule red flame
in unison with the silent skies…
Into what is the metamorphosis
of love, burnt into ashes
and: sinking into the urn,
to be consumed nonchalantly
by the ever-flowing river?
With the glass cocoon broken
each shard bearing the imprint
of the painfully detaching soul
Love becomes a memory.
of beauty and poignance…
The smoke rises high above.

the tavern, where travellers
pine for the lost paradise,
They don't have the eyes.
to see the image of the soul
that too dreamt about love
in a life full of longings;
Beyond the scared pages
of joyful fulfilment
Is the chapter unread?
of genuine love wasted
in the delusion of life;
By the time the barrenness
and futility is apparent
The body has lost the earth,
with just a drop of tears
deposited on the final page,
The fire slowly flares up.
to swallow the scalding tear
along with the last fragment
of the calcified remnants of life,
Love is palmed off with care.
from life to death
by the most ancient of fires
along with the mute sculptures
of the long extinct gods …

The bed behind the bedlam

Within the deception
of physically observed space,
nondescript and shallow
is the unmistakable murmur…
Not the chorus
of the restless people,
But that of the ocean
mighty and calm…
A landless place
of anonymous obscurity,
which once visited
is never forgotten;
An enduring mystery
That is unsolvable
a paint-less painting
with lifelike abstractions!
A rockery with figurines
on which mirrors
the poignant silence
of the all-knowing waters…
A catacomb within,
that has symbolic signs
of elusive prescience
where darkness dwells;
The path is inconspicuous.
by the trodding feet of time,

The cobblestones aged
and shrouded in shrubbery;
What the eyes did not see
and the cognition was ignored
has been entangled
in the labyrinth of the mind,
What has been suppressed
by the bedlam of the day,
is born in the bed
where the child sleeps!
The windows were left half ajar.
with the dancing curtains
in the softest moonlight
let the voices from the other side,
from the parallel world
permeate the half awake ears…
The incognito meanders
along the concealed path
as the narrator recites
the verses of an ancient poem
in the ruins of a forgotten temple;
The shadows of the lost souls
Revisit the world of the living.
vocalising the earthly thoughts
as if they were never dead…
The homeless memories
Find a much-needed respite.
in the myriad imageries
within the tabernacle of grief…
In the sweetness of the lies
frivolous like a fresh blossom,

The truths of life are hidden.
just so that the child could sleep,
Who would wake up as an adult?
to smell the newness of dawn
and cherish the newfound memories,
to wilfully dwell in the falsities,
the poetic beauty of the imagery,
the random collection of which
He would come to call it "a dream…"

A peculiar rain

The gentle wave arose.
from the oceanic skies,
The first rain of a dry spring!
Initially, there were alphabets.
parroted by kindergarten children,
Then they condensed into words.
poetic and aesthetically pleasing,
With infinitesimal permutations
they proliferated with virulent vigour,
paving the way for the long passages
as a new saga was being written!
The rain was especially eloquent.
with its fearlessly fluent fluidity;
Notably absent were the processions,
the pomp and splendour of regality:
No drum beats of exalted winds
No chariots of light pulled by roaring lions
No fiery visual spectacles on display,
Yet, the effect was almost hypnotic.
as the beholder stood by the window
transfixed by the narration by nature!
The sleep wiped the parched soil clean.
brought the smile back to the lips
of the flowers, with their magical touch
perfumes percolated through the bed
imbibing the fascinating floral fragrance!

The trees bathed as nudes in the garden.
as the leaves levitated with the damsels
and the branches played with the drops;
The wave receded as gently as it came.
leaving miniature seas in the gutters
for the ascetic frogs to meditate;
The freshly woven wet robes of greens
atop the satiated fertile farm land
scripted a prologue for the season
concluding with a heartfelt word of gratitude…

The predicament of Dr. Faust

From the shores
of inevitable mortality,
The busybodies strive
to attain dominance,
behaving as if demented
about the chapter of love
that binds the world!
From their darkened space
They scream at the mirrors.
smashing them to smithereens
unable to stand the sight
of the demonic smiles
reciprocating with alacrity
from behind the glass!
From the hollows
of their emptied minds,
The demons emerge alive.
licking the glass shards
with blood on their tongues,
ever so eager for more
their thirst never quenched!
From the occupied rooms
The clones of Mephistopheles laugh
enchanting the entrapped beings,
The loud promises of eternity
the lure of voluptuous desires

and the chance to be super-human
blissfully sweet and tempting…
From the mouths gaped open in wonder.
The souls of Fausts take rebirth,
to be inveigled again by the devils!
To be wilfully corrupted
to abandon the blessing of love
and to be subjugated by hatred,
to make the earth the home of devils…
From the planet of mystery
no living soul goes anywhere,
What is here in the reality of the present
would be something else here tomorrow
another guise, same being…
But the devils play the trickery.
of a conscious existence in eternity,
disarming the victims into submission…

The game of ratios

"Equal parts mad
equal parts sane!"
exclaimed Michael de Montaigne
in a fit of laughter
as the moonlight scintillated
amidst the tower of books;
"Goodness and devilry
In all probability, in equal ratio?"
He fell back into thoughts again.
At best, man is a mix of both,
an animal he is for certain,
regardless of his social rank
Or his soft speaking tongue!
What "is "real is a deception
a delight to behold,
There cannot be a state of "is."
The being is a state of flux,
But man, essentially being human
would surrender to the illusion
without betraying his true self
that is deeply skeptical ...
"It flows,
Not the river's soliloquy
But the thought of Heracles
who sat at the banks
trying to make sense of life

and its dynamic imagery;
"It doesn't",
retorted Piramides
stationed at the opposite shore!
What is flowing to one pair of eyes
is a constant for another,
What is evidently insane for one
could be lucid for someone else…
The change is at the surface
In reality, nothing changes,
What is the pristine river at present
was a lot of snow before
destined to fertilise a land
and feed the people on the banks
with crops of food for their stomachs
and thoughts for their minds …
It is not the assurance of the afterlife
But the certainty of death
that ought to guide humankind,
It is the consciousness
that keeps man on earth,
his perception of the world
and all its inherent complexities
is his vision for life …
The philosophers didn't argue
The faith of one was acceptable
so was the faith of another,
No two pairs of eyes see the same sight
The mount could be an anthill
The geometry of things in nature
is fluid and speculative,

The hill and the river form a unit
complementing each other,
Like the man and his soul
within the shell of absurdities
There is a deeper imprint of the universe,
The world is like the blood circulation
feeding the organs and recycling itself
keeping an intricate dynamics intact
within the apparent prosiness,
As the mind delves into the cell
dissecting every invisible organelle,
a world emerges with startling novelty
opening doors within the darkness
to unlock the mystery of life …
Ironical it is the eccentricity of science
would guide man into the realm of lucidity!
The contraption that's the human body
would pave the way to his salvation,
The chest of drawers within his mind
holds the scrolls of his own destiny,
The future of his own species
depends on his confronting his own devilry
and recognising the true face within him,
He is a sensitive character
within a landscape painting
who feels that the river is flowing,
but to the beholder situated outside
The whole thing is static!
Within the captured moment
everything flows with absolute ease,
After that, the moment ceases to exist

and the flow becomes virtual
in a parallel world with curated memories,
It is within that cryptic world
that man would seek seeds of his sanity…

The annihilated

What's unformed
as yet within the chrysalis
is the corporeal man,
What's inside is the seed
would become the embryo;
But the foetus isn't him,
as he is twice born
First, as an independent organism
and then as the servile creature,
The man in the womb is a myth
He takes his avatar eventually
as an amalgam of absurdities
with a mind full of experiences,
that would reshape his vision
of the world and its tragedies …
The reverse is the metamorphosis
of the man into a moth
that seeks not the light of dawn
But the darkness of the night!
Misleading is the contraption
That's the adulthood of the mind,
masking the selflessness of self
and the trueness of mortality,
Within the incontrovertible truth
The moth sees the bed of immortality
and with the exuberant confidence

That nullifies the pact with reason
The creature races into its destiny
the indifferent, unedifying death
That ends the entropy of the cells
skinning the external garment of life
making the figure in the Sistine Chapel,
Grotesque is the emerging imagery
And truly gruesome is the kill
of the ambitious man within the moth,
dispersing the seed at the core
along with xylem sap of dreams …
Every day in life was a judgement
The gavel has been in his hands,
The judge was none but himself!
How cleverly he had been deceived
by the entrapping gossamer of time!
The clock is a masquerading spider
astutely weaving the web of illusions,
from which there's no escape for man
Once he has unlearned the art
of being an embryo within the womb …
He has heard no prophesying oracles
Nor has he heeded the subtle messages,
The Odysseus in him was bound
to endure pain in the isles of misery,
Yet the theatre of a tempestuous life
with its moralistic trials and tribulations
didn't carve an Übermensch out of the man,
He was to become a nondescript insect,
a vector of his unfulfilled dreams …
It ought to be a seafarer too,

in the ship that set sail from Troy in flames!
Colligated with the living and non-living
is the man with a civilised garb,
a curious creature of contradictions
evolved not just through bloodlines
but by countless streams of dreams
incubated in a world of observations;
Man is a constellation of stars
with an unending desire not to end!
His life is but one shred of reflected light
from the desiccated rocks in the cosmos,
too transitory to be perceptible
But that which has a mind of its own …
As Helen resurrects for the dreamy Faust
He is tricked by the lifelike imageries,
the sacred concepts that he memorised
in the hope of perpetual upmanship,
dominating others as an unnatural being!
The beauteous princess was a myth
The ships are miniatures in the showcase
perched on blue paints of lifeless seas,
as brittle as his imaginative life
and that which doesn't need a storm
but just a passing wind, to be toppled over
and smashed on the merciless ground
to a thousand unknowable pieces!…

Cloud in the cup

Nothing like a cup
of fresh summer rain
to revitalise the spirits,
He thought that moment
as the clouds gathered
and the winds broke free
from the arms of stillness …
The samovar was hot
huffing like the steam train,
The tea would be perfect
But the rain is ethereal
more than perfect, divine!
It's one thing to savour
the sight with delight
as the identical drops sprout
from the aged window sills;
It's a different league altogether
to drink the clouds' concoction,
Having said that to himself
He emptied the teapot
hastening to the verandah
to catch the very first shower!
And it was such a downpour
Unlike any of the previous summers,
The tears of the yesterdays
laced with the hopes of the morrows

formulating a unique rain
that poured from the skies
into the pot and from there
slowly trickled down his throat,
It was so delicately cold
that reminded him of rain
in which he was drenched
Sometime in his childhood,
It felt tender like the petals
of a flower, its name unknown,
It brought tears to his eyes
which he thought were aged and dry…
He hurried back to the room
ensuring no one has witnessed
His adventure on a rainy day!
They wouldn't understand
as they probably don't feel anymore,
Let it be so!
He fell back into his bed
swiftly sinking into a sleep
that he had missed for long …

The stretch

How many miles
Just how many miles
Can one be away
from the place
that he would call his home
or the place that once was
the only home he knew?…
Dishevelled, cold, hungry
gone astray like a cat
How long could he survive
with his home not in sight
and for several unknown miles?…
The rains would be unkind
and the night lonesome
not a friend to open the heart
The birds are gone, eerily quiet
and with no shade to offer shelter
It would be fearful, terrible
an utterly detestable nightmare!
The phantasms do not sleep
Alas! they never do,
as they ain't the diurnal animals
like the wretched displaced man,
they would dance with the gales
and spit flames of lightning
not afraid of the dark

indeed they own the night
encircling the man like gremlins
bent on creating allegories
out of their illusionistic mischiefs!
No, he cannot be so far away
from the place where love dwells,
like a suckling going without milk
He dies inch by inch inside
along with his painful longings,
The trunkless legs of Ozymandias
in the vastness of the desert
remind him of the distance,
the long, impossible track
littered with riddles and hurdles …
Like the ambitious man
who ran into his own death
In Tolstoy's short, intense story
He feels that he's going in a circle
The path is a clever deception
That would keep him away
from what would be
his forever home!…

A day at the heights

Beautiful is the passing day
that mints gold in every sheaf of hay!
It is apropos as long as it feels fine
Life's jaunty like "the hay wain",
So thought the shepherd at heart
as the sun was starting to depart,
He was running his fingers over the lyre
Whilst the song birds made the choir!
The soul of the lake poet in the cloud
whom the daffodils would astound,
whispers lyrics into the youngster's ear
as the voice of one whom he holds dear!
The meadows are fond of the fawns
like the memories of the bygones,
Time is real, but it is rather immaterial
When with nature, life is congenial,
He has water and food in the bag
a simple life about which he wouldn't brag,
A life to be lived, not for any acclaim
win or lose, the end would be the same,
He gazes at the moors and the parsonage
where the three sisters wrote every page
of their awe-inspiring works long ago,
The bells toll like in the poem of Poe
sublime to begin with, then frenetically
to the tunes the daffodils would rally …

Chameleonic is the god of the storms
The breeze could be one of his many forms!
“It changes “is engraved on the tombstone
Again, to borrow the great Poe,” alone”…
In solitude, the universe is profound
where silence is the only sound …
The sun renounces the scintillations
decay naturally happens to all bastions,
The day is passing, the setting is bucolic
The melody from the lyre is melancholic,
But the shepherd has untainted happiness
to him, his space is heaven, not any less …

The dreamy inquiry

It's a question of faith
It always has been
It will always be! …
The enduring mystery of life
is the mystery of dreams,
If one ought to believe in life
He has to trust the dream,
"the illusion within the illusion"
The foetus in the night's womb
is born as the fantasy
Animated caricatures but fully alive
and as real as reality could be!
The intriguing parodies they sing
borrowed from the trivia of life,
the homesickness they instill
in the wistful heart of the dreamer,
the vitality they bestow upon life
that transcends into a new dawn,
They ought to be believed
for they are true but abstract,
fluidly transparent phantasms
masterfully eluding daylight,
sculpting images out of the shadows
that had long been forgotten,
challenging the finitude of time
and the dimensions of space …

The eternalised moments of love
the panacea to the insufferable pain
of grief, and loss that cuts and bleeds
the memory chambers of the heart,
The time capsule created by the dream
is the medicine for pain, the analgesic
that revitalises the failing spirits
of the traveller in the misty woods…
He has to hold onto the visions
of the past unearthed from the moors
of forgetfulness with the seeds sown
for the flowers of hope and newer dreams!
That which has been sidetracked
and even forced to be in oblivion
by the ceaseless humdrums of the world
is reborn in the parallel world of visions,
It isn't the futuristic clairvoyance
but an intricate study of the past itself,
reminding him time and again that
There's an unseen side to the world
He has unfortunately ignored this thus far …
It's not overweening, it's not a mirage
but an adroitly crafted web of illusions
that do demand attention with sincerity …
The man is helpless as he is absorbed
into the magical world as an orderly,
Who is a subject, a narrator in the kingdom
of a long-buried past which is familiar,
Knowing deep inside that it would vanish
at the first touch of the spring sun
leaving his hands empty but his heart full

with a unique stash of hazy visuals,
perceptible yet fragile and often illogical,
to be cherished within the clutter of life
as the skilfully complex art of absurdity,
which strangely translates with ease
into the art of living in the reality of the world …
Like the dew drops on the flower bed
that blurs the concept of consequence,
enhancing the beauty of the earthiness
as if heaven has planted the tears
on the cheeks of the earth with a kiss,
imparting a sight not just to behold
but a thought to be ruminated in the mind,
churned to fineness, to atoms of wisdom,
winnowed from the disorder that's nature,
The blossoms that simply refuse to die
children of the creator that is the mind,
anecdotes of the human experience
antidote to the oddity that is called life,
To be lived over and over again
with a secret passion never to surrender
to the ubiquitousness of timed death
by dreaming, dreaming and nothing else,
for the helpless man to be the tiny drop of dew
on the effervescent face of the earth,
the atom of a dream, that knows not
where it has its roots to which it returns …

A windy evening

I saw the air swell
A chasm of invisibility
and infinite probabilities
had surrounded me,
that too all of a sudden …
With the sun gone down
and the birds nowhere to be seen,
All that was there was the murmur
of a wind that foretold a rain
inevitable in the insufferable heat …
Beyond that, it was just me
the only human being on earth
The wingless creature perched
on a slithery twig of hope;
That is how it felt at heart
Though I knew I was a traveller
beholding the prelude to a summer rain,
The first movement begins in earnest
opening the symphony of nature,
The attentive audience included
the red blooms of the flame tree
and the man walking his dog,
The latter settled on the leafy track
while the flowers nodded their heads,
With the wind that is so perceptible
like the rhythm of the heartbeat

A wave of inexplicable emotions arose
as if the sea of floating leaves
belonged to the distant past …
Man gets transfixed in a trance
When the space expands around him
not with the spectacle of sprites
or fantasies of flamboyant colours,
But in the most elemental of experiences
He too becomes a natural phenomenon,
an element, an atom that seeks its ties
with the discarded cradle of birth …
As time randomly flows backwards
a feeling of impending tears
comes to the liquid black eyes,
I feel like crying, as if I'm a suckling
orphaned and seeking shelter,
Though it isn't stormy or raining, as yet…
I could only wish that the wind
would levitate me to the cobwebbed loft
where I could grab the rag doll
and stay there in hiding, buried by memories,
as if the leaky roof was the eternal sky!…

Reflecting on the waters

I see the reflections
of the waters on the ceiling
Light, the master sculptor
chisels out figures from fluids
and solids with great facility!
The curated works of morning shine
convert the ground into a gallery
of geometrically precise art,
the wondrous illusions of optics,
For the discerning eyes
to savour with delight, the spontaneity
of the prolific creativity of nature,
in silence and relative obscurity …
One could affix metaphors
or find profound meanings
in the changing patterns of light
Or indeed unearth nothing at all,
But the feeling is perceptible
that the world is a showcase
of the waltzing rays of light!
Man is, perhaps, a tiny, flimsy wall
in the massive gallery of nature
for the fingers of light to draw
and dig deep into the heart,
bridging the chasm that separates
Reality and the ever-elusive mirage

to make some sense of the phantasms
that encircle the cast away soul ...
The flower pot doesn't know
its reflection in the febrile waters,
The image doesn't really know
The man on the other side of the mirror!
Thoughts originate from nowhere
like the rains and the winds, to disappear
and to reincarnate as dreams,
The air is a sea of scattered illusions
that the eyes simply cannot see,
Nature translates the invisibility
to tangible imageries on the wall,
Thoughts are alive in the magnificence
of the ceilings of the chapel,
playing with the light of a new dawn
and the pale shadows of the past ...
The world is recreated every moment
by the flux in human consciousness,
"I" is more than what's seen by the eye
The sense of being, the feeling of existing
is the thought from the passing light
that carves philosophy out of physics,
poetic images of the subconscious,
the art of the dream, the gift of nature ...

Reading a cryptic scroll

The resistance comes from within
through the dark echo chambers
not to forget and surrender!
The exhorting voice is strong
The intention slowly becomes clear
not to be subdued by the callous time
and be mercilessly sunk into oblivion …
The random tests are calibrated,
The candidate has no choice
but to participate in the trial
dreading deeply that he would lose …
The examiner is a martinet
His stern eyes were tickling with mischief
the same fear, the same anxiety
grips the vain examinee's mind
just so that he wouldn't forget
The many travesties of reality!
Every passing character is a symbol
The key to the world of abstractions
Dream is, after all, a visual language
that cannot be written down
or illustrated with clarity on paper …
The memorised formula is elusive
hiding behind the pine trees of time,
He is impelled to pursue the loss,
The ground can't be trusted anymore

as the leaves hide pits of darkness …
The dream is a testament to human vanity
the fragile imageries of a lauded life
brazenly exposed for the soul to see
like the exegesis of an ancient scroll,
Even the alluring colours of dawn
can't mask the impact on the mind …
The lies are in cahoots with the truths,
their numbers and significance are uncertain,
The faces must be pleading for eternity
as the fog of falsified memories looms large
over the terrains of fervent imagination …
The characters ought to be protesting
against the perceived injustice of time,
as the graves are dug in an alien space
to bury them alive, whilst still breathing …
The dream is a renegade act
to symbolise the agitation of the mind
that refuses to be subjugated by finitude,
If only the departed souls could tell the man
that they still dream after bodily expiry,
and that they see not the glory of the heavens
but the earthly idylls of love and loss
It would have consoled the dreamer,
who hinges on the hopes of redemption
by reading the intricate engravings
in the hitherto unexplored caves of the mind …

Occult

God, state & the man!
In a flick of a second
He's reincarnated as a god,
a prehistoric minor one,
the forgotten celestial
in the time warp of mythology,
Who can no longer pretend
that he's dead forever …
The state he has been deprived of
is rebuilt from scratch
within the confines of obscurity,
where he would be reinstalled
on the pedestal he had hoped for,
as the insignificant god as of old,
the reliable purveyor of blessings
in return for perfumed offerings,
One amongst the very many,
a marionette at the fingertips
of the clients and their importunes,
who has no sense of reason
But is impelled to act as divine
pulling off one miracle after another!
It all happened in a moment
as the man shuts his eyes with devotion
to pawn his reason for favours,
uttering the empty words of his forbears

to appease the muted deity
believing and praying that's all true!
The fictional skies wept for him
tears of eternal benevolence,
The winds began a poetic discourse
mirroring the words of his heart,
All that the microcosm has is "him",
the man, his state, and his god
all within the subjective consciousness
of a singular person in a chaotic world …
All the events began and ended
within a fractured segment of time,
man becoming his own god
and inversely, in a leap of creativity,
even imagining the dilemma of nature
within the spectacular theatrics
of a prayer, to prove his relevance
and to devise his own destiny…

The gramophone

The auguries of the future
are seeded within a dream,
So too are the travesties
and joys of the bygones
engraved in the dark caverns,
as the enchanting symphony
of visuals and voices reverberates
within the inveterate dreamer …
The vinyl record plays
breaking the eons of silence
in the long forgotten room
as the solemnity of twilight
softly paints the mouldy walls …
It's the music of memories
The sonata in the forbidden space
Whilst a child crawls on all fours
on the remnants of the floor
as if he is an unforeseen rebirth,
brought forth into a timeless zone
which bears the footprints
of what's yet to happen …
There used to be a life, a human one
within the confines of that room,
as the sun melts like a candle
darkness ushers in the tenants
that are none but the shadows

of the phantasms that abound
in such a forsaken place of yore …
Like the cells of the body changing
to be attuned with the passage of time,
The music assumes a nocturnal tone,
the fiery subtlety of melancholy …
It's where man becomes a sprite
in the forest of cluttered visions,
a nameless luminous firefly,
a tearless toddler acutely aware
of his being a hapless orphan
lost in the submerged street
of a forgotten civilisation…
The memory of the future
is the premise of his lonely dream
the semi-transparent fluid miasma
of hidden longings and possessions …
The unwanted sons and daughters
of the mind of loneliness
redeem their right to live
in the distorted space of reality
where the past and the future
unite with the infinity of memories …

Faithfully yours

How faithfully a man would invest
the entire breaths in his chest
seeking the ever-elusive truth
like an astute sleuth!

Every moment in every single year
rekindles his hopes to be nearer
to the times that have been lost
to make peace with his ghost!

He lives in the mirage of the present
with thoughts he yearns to vent,
to break loose from the warp of time
that stays stubborn all the same …

Emboldened by the experiences
of hypnagogia haunting his senses
He meanders like a sloth in his sleep
sinking into the forest in deep …

The reflections are a stir in the skies
The captivating illusion never dies,
The chrysalis resurrects every moment
indubitably finite yet piquant …

Love is vibrant within the hourglass
knowing the time would come to pass
when it is translated into a memory
that would be deified in all its glory …

Restless is the world of the living man
that has neither a creator nor a plan,
The misery of one is the wisdom of another
The seeds in the flower bed sprout together …

Insufferable is the engulfing darkness
the melancholy of the nocturnal dress,
The bells toll at a great distance
signposting to the imaginary lands …

The facade has the permanence of beauty
Absurdity mirrors the shadows of truth!
The train of thought suddenly derails
The lights dim, and the experiment fails...

The soul of the alchemist is the desert
without which he can't play his part
in the chaotic world of madness
The truth ought to be unearthed under duress!…

Beyond the atom

Does ZERO exist?
The boundless eternity,
life with its plenitude of variety,
the perception of joy and pain,
the melancholy of blue art,
the rhythmic chorus of the seas,
the vitality of a spring morning,
the symphony of the songbirds
the mortal remnants of the passing day,
the monochrome imageries of the night,
the warm phlegmatic breaths of life,
the sighs of unforeseen despair,
Do any of these exist, in reality?
Is there anything called reality?
What is life without the circumstances
the invisible bridges of relationships
bonded by blood and friendships,
and even the strangeness of anonymity!
Once the bridges are incinerated
and the living cells vaporised,
What remains of the so-called life?
He doesn't exist anymore as he's unseen
the one who could exist invisibly
beyond the realms of the human senses
ought to be beyond nature,
Which implies that nature itself

is an assimilation of perceptions
of the living …
The brain that has closed the receptacles
of multidimensional sensory impressions,
is opaque to the perception of reality;
But could it be true
that the abstruse would still exist
in a continuum of time?
Could it be true
that beyond the finitude of death
There is the certitude of the afterlife,
that even the dissipated soulful energy
isn't conscious about,
As consciousness exists only in the living
And what happens thereafter is as obtuse
as the concept of ZERO …

Conversations with a doll

You're
that singular broken thought
of a meditative universe,
You're
that panel of curious shapes
in an irrevocably forgetful dream
You're
the fruit of a miserable evolution
in a mendacious world
You're
the epicentre of subjective reality,
a spurious object in nature
You're
the soul that seeks immortality
a suckling that can never be free
You're
the transience of the evening shine
the eternal lover of darkness
You're
the writer of a tale of woes
with poignant blood-tinged words
You're
not bound to know certitude
The vagabond on a perilous terrain
You're
the stoic seed of volatile insanity

the bird caged within a thoughtful dream !...
You're
that which exists in the matrix of time
distinctive from that which doesn't exist

You're
The second that has fallen off the dial
the lone satellite of the impassive clock
You're
the songbird that knew not itself
nor the destiny yonder at the horizon
You're
the plaything of a cantankerous god
extant only within you, the orphan child ...

The teller of time

Tomorrow has happened (as we speak)
So has the day after!
His voice is prophetic,
The horologist is quietly confident
Whilst dissecting a specimen of time
on his eternally dusty table
with a smirk of nonchalance;
The boy's eyes grew wider
his chest heaving with curiosity,
as the bespectacled furrowed eyes
teased out the mysterious ailment
from the circle of vanishing seconds …
"The *whole* is not the sum of its parts,
Is that true? …"
He queried with utmost eagerness
subjecting the philosophy lesson to test,
The old man raised his eyebrows
mirroring the curiosity back at him
I only wish I knew...
said a murmur of saintly words
as he fell back into his surgical work;
The boy wandered into the table of time
like a cake sliced and apportioned
to be partaken with diligence
by the guests of the world,
Each modicum with a purpose

every moment like a drop of liquid
that would choose not to stay
but collapsing into the abyss of the unreal
at the intercourse of time and memory …
The unassuming clock at its finest mutation
may know the realm of infinity,
the melange of the ticking times
feels rhythmic to the human mind
But maybe chaotic for the universe …
If impermanence is the rule of life
The biological clock diluted into nothingness
Time, too, is relevant only whilst alive?
When the man dies
and the path of the soul cleared
time too would die with him,
His clock stopped from within,
Is that true after all?…
The soul could be an expansion
of the time not yet experienced,
a fragment of timelessness?
That would mean
that immortality is within the man
and not somewhere in the heavens?
"*What on earth am I thinking!*"
The boy came back to his senses
realising he must have grown older
in a malleable scale of time
whilst playing with the abstractions
that haunted the room like apparitions!
And in that hole in the wall,
all the while with a mischievous smile

The old man seemed engrossed
in a delicate act of correcting time …

The shadow of a summer moon

The shadows paced madly
along the rugged corners
of the aged, crumbling wall,
Oblong figures with a monstrosity
too palpable to be ignored!
Wicked-faced phantasms
of the sleepless mind,
the disturbing hallucinations
The seafarer feared lost!
They laugh, they play tricks
from the scroll of some ghoul,
phantoms that spring from the mortar
tease the roller doors of the eyes
with their illusionistic devilries …
An unusually full moon
shot a sardonic grin at the windows,
the placid whiteness of light
contrasted starkly with the figures
in the slithery hours of the night!
"The white face of damnation"
As the great literary mind puts it,
could be lurking in those shadows,
So the mind thinks, or "half-thinks. "
about the abstruse, eerie things,
The allegories created by the light
within the caverns of the soul …

The windows are transparent
letting in the unfettered spectres
dancing to the tunes of primitivity,
grotesque yet queerly amusing
in the fantastic imaginary lands
of essentially human somnolence!
He can't help but let them dance
vainly keeping his eyes half shut,
half thinking, half dreaming,
unsettled and languidly awake
rooting for the orphaned dream
of that suckling who once nestled
in the shade of an eternal mother …

The bend

Whenever he meets him
in the corner, where
The row of shops ends
and a line of smoky houses
arise like awakened corpses,
The afternoon gets dark
and clouds gather from nowhere,
as the dead leaves waltz around,
A cold nocturnal embrace
envelops his slender frame
and a foreboding of the uncertain
chokes his frivolous mind …
He is none but his "double. "
a duplicitous non-entity
a symbolism of his alter ego
who takes his sudden avatar
from ethereal space, it seems!
In between them, there is nothing
no shield of broken glass
that would reflect the souls
suspicious about each other,
But the interlude of the wind
has the gist of a raging storm;
They simply stare at each other
as if they hadn't met before,
transfixed like two candles

glued by their melting feet!
The silence cuts in deep
burrowing holes in the confidence
of the man, the protagonist,
The frozen eyes of the other
spell out the sinister intentions
with surprising candidness,
Behind the thick towel of smog
that wraps around the metropolis
with no other souls in sight,
The two stand a few feet apart
but caged in a singular vortex
where only one would survive
becoming the master of "the other "...

The banal aberration

In the goodness of a few
The banality of evil
would be neutralised?
The spiritual allure of goodness
versus the pragmatism of evil
forms the crux of the dichotomy
of the peculiar gene
that makes one human …
The world of a few people
may have been uniformly good,
Inherent is the kindness and love
that bond one man with another?
The chaotic sphere of billions
is the vortex of countless neuronal fires
in which the sanctity of nobility
collapses into a painful absurdity!
Paramount is the survival
Sacro-sanct is the genetic encumbrance
to thrive and be the progenitors
passing down the biological code
as expected of a natural being;
Enthralling is the charm of power
to dictate and subjugate,
Wickedly amusing is the thrill
that some gain at inflicting pain,
The wild-eyed beast cruelly smiles

from behind the naked gene,
in every soul born into the species!
Man could devise a civilisation
knit together a fine society
create dogmas of virtuousness
pursue lofty ideas of philosophy
and the manifold wonders of science,
making the world a livable place
where the health of the collective counts
improving upon the past with ingenuity
and an unflinching passion for life,
which makes the cerebral sapien
a monumental marvel!
But within that intricate network,
In the evolved institution, namely the society
There is the idiosyncratic individual,
whose moral tenet is an uncanny mixture
of highly subjective good and evil,
which means his sieve is one of practicality
and what best suits his inner desires,
He isn't fearful of Dante's circles of hell
or moved by Bosch's Garden of Earthly Delights
The one human he loves the most
is none but himself!
Above all, he is aware of his predicament
In choosing between self-love and empathy
The opportunist in him opts for the former
Indulgence being his simple theory of life!
The sapien's reform can only happen
from deep within his heart,
Goodness ought to be filtered out

only after his cognisance of the evil,
The more he avoids the truth
The deeper he sinks into the marshlands
of fractured hopes and unrequited love …
He isn't amenable to redemption
through any force of a holy decree
His romance with death is primordial
And his aversion to truth is an inborn instinct; life thrives on
the nourishment of lies
with an untold affinity towards what's evil,
Even if life is safeguarded with certitude
and destiny is as clear as the day
man would still be cynical,
He doubts the innocence of goodness
which he regards as the sacrilege
of what is unabashedly adored in his mind
secretly, away from the peering eyes,
the ubiquitous unnoticeable evil …
That which keeps him brooding over
is the passiveness of goodness
contrasted with the sheer force
of what's assumed to be evil;
Violence is truthful in its hatred
unhinged in its passion to conquer
while the unassuming benevolence
is diluted in a sea of anonymity …
His fatal obsession with finality
underlies the magnetism of darkness,
The night is one deep long cave
in which he would be that caveman again
fearful, but spirited and adventurous

to overcome his own insufferable dread!
In the cold eyes of the hypnagogic incubus
and the demonic smile of Mephistopheles
He sees his own darkness,
the fragility of his presumptive morality,
The lions stare and gnarl at Daniel
The demons are within, alive and counting
The stone steps man ought to go down
to be a resident of the earthly hell,
to become one amongst the many
with an insatiable, vile urge
to be the most evil in the crowd,
who breaks the bounds of sanity
to be absorbed into the darkness
to be the pathological microbe
the wildest storm that wreaks havoc
on the species of his sad birth …

The unending brook

Stand by the brook
to hear the filibustering
of the minuscule ripples!
Take a seat on the boulder
to see the scared hare
hopping into oblivion,
the cold fingers of winter
balding the cottonwoods,
the phantasms that've existed
from the dreams of the dead
meandering in the wilderness
and the moss grew over
the footprints of a shepherd …
Keep your ear to the ground
to listen to the silent eruptions
of the volcanoes underneath
the veneer of the idyll,
Blindfold the eyes, to gently feel
the illusion of stillness of time,
The prescience of dynamism
of inevitable changes in the offing
fills the caverns of the mind
as a perfect juxtaposition
to the image of uncorrupted beauty …
The sense that the lexicon is empty
to describe the finer details

of the simplest of imageries in nature
instigates the urge for poetry
as the rhythm of the flow
goes in cahoots with the tunes
of the liquid in incessant motion …
The randomness of occurrences
disrupts the connections of patterns
rendering a novelty to the experience
and an indescribable pall of melancholy;
He has been on those rocks before
But that was beyond his awareness,
a nascent moment that was
too randomly furtive an occurrence
to fit into the mould of memory;
The brook is a fragment of his conscience
a looking glass with many a shard
waiting for the moment to break apart
and pierce the silence like stilettos
peeling the mask of the countenance
that would replicate as a dream
in which he would be the beholder
of the spectacle of illusory sprites,
decoying the man into the jungle
of jumbled memories where all is still
and the dread of darkness lingers …

The glass

The glass stays idle
the volume of water untouched
without the human thirst
to be essentially quenched
to rejuvenate the spirit of life!
The wind and the invisibles
cast away in oneiric isles
trundle along the leafy bundles
the tombs of the withered ones,
as the pallid moon in the clouds
glances at the uneasy shadows
creeping behind the tall pines;
The glass is unperturbed
with no life to be satiated,
The volume is precise
The water inside is meditative,
the nocturnal blue aura
augments the unearthly silence
creating an accoutred image
of the longings of a long night …
The belief in absolute stillness
would be shaken to the core
if even a drop is amiss,
As physical energy is the prerequisite
to move and change matter,

The cellar is buried deep in the cave
beneath the icicles of fantasy,
where the water is in a state of unrest
and the darkness is pernicious,
where the visions are distorted
revealing convoluted by-paths
like the countless limbs of a spider!
The bottles weep in silence
crimson tears descend through the walls
painting strange, rugged images
reminiscent of the extinguished bodies
pining over what has been lost ...
The glass is unshakeably stoic
The rebellion in deep is imperceptible,
The surface is neat and tidy
without much room for afterthoughts,
The vestiges of life were wiped away
by the astute hands of time ...
The trickling of submerged thoughts
penetrate the darkness within
as the moon appears over the cellar
lighting up the single window
throwing glimpses of the grotesque art
evolving lucidly on the walls,
translating allegories of the ancients
into a mysterious script of intricate optics ...
The dreamer sees the fragmented bones
The glass retains the flesh intact,
In the interface of life and life after
The night dissolves into a shadowy mist
Whilst the glass awaits newer life

to emancipate it at dawn
from the shackles of stillness …

Durer's hare

The duopoly of the real and unreal
is challenged by the dream,
There it exists
in its own infinite space
A fascinating panoply of images
forming a beguilingly cogent story!
The characters are nocturnal beings
thriving in the daylight of a dream,
interposed in the imaginative spectrum,
Living and breathing in another world
where definitive dimensions dissolve
in the pond of elevated consciousness,
A newer subspecies of the sapiens
evolving amongst the entangled memories
to enact and interact with playfulness
reminiscing about the buried benign romantic
whilst spotlighting the darker side
of being human …
The drama is akin to a mock drill
trialling and erroring with crafty scenarios
to test the resilience of the mind
with derivative woodcuts from real life;
In tandem with the passing hours
The parallel world expands its bounds,
tugging at the dormant strings at heart
to perceive the deeper subconscious

and a pastiche of reality within surrealism!
There comes alive Dürer's unassuming hare
after centuries of enigmatic, bewitching stare,
to burrow into the labyrinth of imageries
enticing the mind to follow the concealed trail
eventuating in the third act, where the mirrors reflect
a thousand faces of Alice in Netherworld!…
The oneiric sphere is like an onion
peeling itself skilfully layer by layer
The tempo of intrigue builds to a climax
to release the pent-up emotions and desires
where the moth-eaten dolls come alive
and the tallow candle shines bright
in the loft of half-forgotten memories …

Lamentation

The leaves are papers
on which love is scripted
wrapped in tearful dew …
Every inch of the path
is etched with the transience
misty with poignant longings;
Whose conspiracy is life,
the minefield of illusions
ready to blow up hopes
into shreds of vanity!
Is life swindled out of earth
into the den of the afterlife,
a thievery of the unknown?
Who knows
And what's the point in knowing,
when everything is determined
by the collusion of randomness?
Around the nucleus of happenings
Life faithfully orbits as a satellite,
reflecting the enchanting light
of profound insights …
The unpredictability of chance events
has an element of godliness (?)
Behind the sadness of misfortune
is an erroneous moment,
the fractional second of time

that would forever be elusive
in the plague of insanity;
Cocytus, the river of wailing
is flooded with human tears,
No other animal weeps so profusely
for those lost forever in Hades;
From the cold marble tombs
The ion of immortality is sought
knowing it is beyond a human,
As after all he is a plain leaf …
The leaf should be dead
dry, discarded, dismembered
with a faint print of its veins
remaining as a memory,
fragile, prone to falsehood,
but lovable till the end of eternity …

A superstition nevertheless

Life's man's
most stubborn superstition...
The beginning and the end
are celebrated alike,
A grand welcome
and a solemn send-off
That's the traditional ritual!
The story would've been read
no page left unturned
every word put to scrutiny
and logical exercises,
Yet, beyond the third act
is the afterword
that can never be read,
Before the origins
is the ineffable prologue
nothing but a misty mirage ...
In the two unseen chambers
is encrypted the gist of life,
The space within a lifespan
is one of relentless thoughts,
inferences and reconciliations,
that find their expressions
through language and art;
There are infinitesimal possibilities
and a man's life secures just one,

to think, act, repent
rejoice, replicate, weep, and die …
The embalmed, perfumed body
is a cage within a glass cage,
with rigid sinews and an absent soul
Not a drop of tear does the body shed
over the loss of its own life,
It exists only as far as
The brain and the heart agree,
The rest is imaginative
That sounds true, feels so real,
Yet, man doesn't know
as long as he's alive,
For he's a fragile foetus
that knows not the language
and the intellectual armour of mankind,
He's a novice to every new dawn
reborn through endless dreams,
where he meets the departed souls
wading into the deep tunnels
through the broken waters of birth
where memories come alive
and death defies the dictums of time …
It's his fate, nature's decree
that he should endure the pain of life,
burying his longings in the blind trust
of an afterlife and redemption,
The superstition is beyond reason
which the mind is accustomed to,
The fixation on the permanence
and the fear of transience

bleed his heart and torment him,
yet, like the clenched fist of a newborn
He holds on to that "something."
that's neither a matter nor a hope
but a shred of eternity!
As if the boundless fantasies of life
have been elemental in him
even before his beginning …
If only he could catch a glimpse
of those two pages
that constantly evade his senses,
He wonders,
His life would've been different,
but at risk of losing its alluring aura
within the unbreakable glass of predictability,
like a body within a coffin …

The fourth act

The third act of the warbling birds,
the decrescendo of the symphony
suffuse with ease into the indigo skies,
auguring the birth of the night,
The evening vow of raging summer
gets crickets in the emerging light
of the elegant crescent moon ...
The emancipated souls of the withered flowers
seeking the wandering redeemer in the clouds,
the feathers of the luminescent star
swept over by the winds into oblivion,
The gnomes in the abandoned yard
that are the remnants of the future,
the monuments of murdered memories
the fearful anxieties of an apocalypse,
the reluctance in facing the looking glass
in the dread of seeing incendiary dreams,
the veinlets of hope in the ancient garden
and likewise every moment from every ion of time
swarming into the cocoon of a single night
to transcend the man into the illusion
that he exists in a microcosmic absoluteness
though imperceptibly transient and unreal ...
He wakes up in a dream, like a sapling
seeking light, he follows the shadows,
the multitude of symbolic interactive images,

to be one amongst them, in that world
where the visual storytelling is sublime;
All the while he is being himself,
playing out unseen facets of his persona,
fascinated by the resurrection of the lost times
reliving in the space at the home of his origins,
With ease, he transcends into the foreign lands
where ancient pillars of stone stand in silence,
going past which, he would see his friend
cloistered in the bubble of another story …
The images come off the shelf of memories
to be intertwined with the brave new world
In the planet of timeless imagination!
The house is cluttered with possessions
but it is peaceful, harmonised with the mind,
Children of varying ages thrive in their
playing hide and seek with the dream;
The abstract reflection of what has been seen
re-emerges as a visual motif, an afterthought
that seeks redemption through the dreamer's eyes …
The endless street becomes a tunnel,
the house a burrow and the man a rabbit
with human instincts for relentless pursuit
of the memories reborn as phantasmagoria
with elements of half-revealed truths;
As the man dreams, sharing his imagination
with the gigantic contraption of time,
newer memories ensue, vibrant and almost real
adding a chapter of imaginative introspection
to the unbound compendium of dreams …

The fall

"Let it go,
so that it stays."
says the wise one…
Man clutches with desperation
not just his own life
but that of others too,
hoarding his high hopes
in the dreams of his offspring,
praying for miraculous magic
to catapult his family to fortune
to be rich and be powerful,
and to aspire for even more
so that his coffers are mountainous
from the zenith of which
He could penetrate the clouded skies
and enter the grand heavenly doors
as an unbeaten king, nothing less!
In order that life isn't monotonous
He's enslaved to monstrous ambitions
That would see the fallen angel
waking up, hideously smirking within him,
When man turns into an inhuman beast
The forgotten myth acquires wings of reality,
The eternal slave of passions is violent
a vector of the disease of temptations,
that carves out a netherworld of misery,

self-torment and the void of hopelessness,
As love is butchered mercilessly
and compassion tactically scapegoated
to satiate the insatiable desires,
viciously propagating the cycle of chaos
completing his self-destruction and downfall…
What would be the colossal tragedy
of a man who couldn't perceive love
and the inherent beauty of life,
irrevocably sinking as a painful sight
into the wormholes of darkness …

A grave mistake

Man must've been created
by the confusion amongst the gods
For within him,
is the pure darkness of evil
and the madness of delusions;
He's a renegade,
who rages against goodness
and duels with his own shadow,
He admires his other side in secret
dreaming of devilry to destabilise
the established equilibrium of the world;
The spiteful man from the underground
the nihilist who despises everyone
and finds redemption in his own darkness,
The man who abhors morals and negates society
He knows not the qualm of conscience
and his apathy with deeply ingrained self-love
is the vortex of destruction, beastly and violent,
by which he would play with the creators
maliciously grinning at the muteness of divinity …
To him, his deviant, devilish display too is an art
painted in the crimson of blood and the ashes of carnage,
The gods must've been sleeping during creation
and they're still immersed in the ocean of sleep,
Man hates the silence; the sadism ought to be loud
the wailings of sufferers rivalling those in hell,

The morally corrupted being who can think
knows well the gravity of his cruel misdeeds
But the lure of monstrous villainy is irresistible
His thirst is insatiable even with rivers of blood …

The art of eulogy

One day
You wouldn't wake up
to write anything
not even a single word,
But they would inscribe
(as though) on your behalf
their own thoughts about you
as they're the survivors
and you, the dead!...
They would read out kind words,
prayerfully propitiate with passion
for the soul's propinquity to the god(s),
Would you hear them? No
Would you see their tears? No
Would you find it consoling? No ...
For you would no longer matter
but a heap of ashes or worm food,
Your microcosm ends with your last breath
The doors shut as the pupils dilate,
You would no longer have a life
to be anxious about
You wouldn't have another death
to be fearful about,
In that sense, you would be free? Yes
A resounding yes
that would echo all around,

In the mountains, you never climbed
and the valleys you've never been to,
You would be a memory
accessible to all except yourself,
The world that exists in your consciousness
would be blanketed by darkness,
impenetrably opaque for a mortal,
The delusional dramatics of life
assumes a layer of divinity with death,
as only the soul has the eyes to see god(s),
(thus goes the belief),
So they would say
You were kind and generous
honourable and sorely missed,
knowing not the charade means nothing
to the one who is not alive anymore,
If only
They could be kind to you
share their love for you
whilst you were breathing (like them)
with a lively beating heart (like them)!
But, alas!
They simply pretend they're blind
or behave like some obscurantists
who hide their awareness of love,
reducing you to a verse on a stone instead
that holds no innate meaning
to a man who is asleep forever …

Behind the glass

God created hectically,
then fell into a deep sleep
and never woke up,
The entity isn't dead
not alive either,
but suspended in a dream
fathomless and immersive,
where man is a particle
inconspicuous in the cosmos …
Is man too dead?
and simply dreaming he's alive
him being intellectually endowed
but bereft of the vital sense
to winnow reality from myths?
He could well be a corpse
submerged in the waters
of a weltering dream,
his soul unperturbed
by the plethora of happenings,
But an element of vitality
that's vouchsafed within him
instinctively reacting
to what it believes is true …
Life in itself is a belief
that only has circumstantial evidence,
the man seeing himself in the mirror

is conscious and alive,
if the mirror sees the man
with the latter being unaware
of his own reflection,
Then he must be dead …
The man who is ambulant,
vocalising his thoughts
to be seen and heard by others
ought to be pulsating with life,
The anecdotal records say so!
In other words
the life of a man
is in the perception by the senses
of others,
The mirror has no mind of its own
the property of the matter
is to reflect the figure,
The man raises his hand
and the image reciprocates,
He smiles voluntarily
getting the impression
of the beauty and depth of his expression,
Part of life is in awareness
that one is breathing, in pain or otherwise,
If he pretends to be a log of wood
and believes strongly that he is dead
He might as well be,
at least in his consciousness,
If the others think he's mad
or possessed of something sinister
their minds would conjure up the reasons

to reinforce their own belief!
The particle in an endless dream
has an expansive self
the realm of consciousness
that reflects the universe,
It is volatile, turbulent
prone to catastrophes
in the web of nightmarish thoughts,
the same thoughts that would make it
would eventually be its destruction …
The particle has flesh and bones
and eternally vibrant atoms of thoughts,
It is a man,
hopeless, aggrieved, wretched,
the demonic presence in the god's dream!…

The distance of light

Wake me up!
When the bell rings
announcing the penultimate scene,
before the curtains fall
obliterating the vision forever …
Take me on board
the raft on moonlit waters
where memories die
and newer ones are born
from the pain and blood of grief;
The night silently births the visuals
as the dreamer sits with a reed
hoping to catch a shoal of fish!
Wake me up!
He screams from inside
but there's none to heed his pain,
If only they could hear him,
He could journal the nocturnal visions
and draw the mysterious faces,
emancipating the haunting voices
to make sense of the drama,
As the truth turns even more abstract
The wave transformation happens inside
the man, who, without his dream,
is an inert, inconspicuous animal …
Wake me up!

The voice is muzzled with despair,
The walls of nature are unmoved
The doors decisively shut
The umbilical cord is wrapped tightly
to ascertain the stillness of the newborn!
The realm of dreamy consciousness
buried within the falsities of reality
drifts further away as an isle
that's inaccessible to the mortal …
Wake me up!
He bangs on the doors in anguish
in tears and searing pain at heart,
only to be received by the echoes
of his own lost childhood,
the poignant sight of sinking paradise
reminding him about the tragedy of life …
He dreams so passionately
that he is bound to forget the gist,
to grapple with the fear of uncertainty
within the vortex of real happenings
that would enshroud his life in clouds,
incarcerating him in the darkness
like the chained ingenuous Prometheus,
rebelling against formidable ignorance
with a fennel stalk of light!…

The "Y" in You ...

Does the way know you?
The convoluted path
slithers away into the mist,
painting the illusion of a saint
meandering into the deep
in another locus of time ...
The image emerges from within,
the abstraction of intrigue
and the anticipation of mystery
cohesively forming a reflection
in the stoic pond of thoughts
as if sliced out of a dream!
He has been there forever
You've been there before,
The path whispers that to the air
which transits it to the ears,
You wonder who's the beholder
The illusion regards you in silence
as another illusion, taped to reality...
The future talks to the past
through the medium of the present,
You happen to be here
through a strike of randomness,
Chance, luck (good or ill)
has brought you here to be a witness,
Between you and the weltering fog

Are the unmarked buried skeletons
of the rich and the famous,
fossils of plain humans, expired lives
tabernacles of pieces of history …
You are reminded that the world
is one giant cemetery
and an incubator of new lives,
That which doesn't exist
is a calcified remnant of an illusion,
a curated memory, transient though …
Consciousness refers back to the past
the wealth of experiences and anecdotes
to decipher the meaning of the image,
by reading into the enchanting silence
to collate the verbiage of nature
to arrive at a believable conclusion,
which affirms faith in your own sanity
within the gossamer of mirrored reflections …
The path exists within that matrix
of painful longings and suppressed wishes,
It knows you, mirroring your own knowledge,
It doesn't exist without you,
the living fossil, the perpetual dreamer,
the aficionado of abstract symbols,
the digger of the memory graves of the past
who strives to find his meaning within himself …

The transcendence

When does the bird
Become a fly?
When it wings farther away
dissolving into the distance,
Whilst the eyes are static
striving to make sense of
the inverted visual inputs …
Democritus laughs aloud
within the universe of atoms
bearing the truth of life,
The units in perpetual motion
that impart the impression of living;
The bird "flies" into the fly,
The fly transcends into invisibility
in the farthest copse and beyond
attaining the realm of non-existence,
to be initiated into the mirage of memories
immune to visual capture
but perceptible as a transient life,
a flutter, a moment in motion …
The fiery stone of Anaxagoras,
the godless sun burns unto death,
imploding like the human minds
not knowing the purpose of the flame,
As precious life contradicts itself
through the travesties and conflicts;

The randomness of atomic events
makes every living being equal,
The accomplishments are ephemera
rewarding but ultimately meaningless,
All that's here is in the moment
When the cold, rocky moon exudes poetry
in the peace of the dreaming night,
When man seeks succour in thoughts
within the cauldron of imagination,
It is vested with him to create anew
reflecting on the harrowing phantasms
in the context of eventual nothingness;
The Kafkaesque vermin awakened,
taking flight along the trajectory
of the unshackled bird yonder,
at liberty, to find atoms of truth …

“Man” mal

Man is a peculiar mirror
in that he looks into himself
and the glass reflects the same
in whatever he sees around him;
The externalisation of the inner image
though hazy and intricately abstract
skews every inch of his perception
like the mist shrouding the woods…
Thus, there are really no “others.”
but varied versions of his own self,
The urge to love is counterpoised
by the vile instinct of hatred!
No wonder the intellect is futile
when he makes evidently bad choices,
His gumption augurs progress
Yet he can be stunningly foolish,
All thanks to the mirror that’s him;
The images become so overpowering
that he suspects his own sanity
as they cloud his consciousness
dismantling him into minuscule segments
That would be reflected back
creating a slave out of the master
who can no longer trust himself …
There is water in the pond as well as the sea
Humanity exists even in the inhuman

Though so diminutive that it isn't visible …
But his basic sanity is dubitable,
prone to demonic outbursts of rage,
as the beast thrives in the shadows
of the shattered smiling images of himself …
He is nothing but a mammal
solipsistic, egoistic, subdued by survivalism;
His own desire and craving for pleasure,
his grudge and the enticement of revenge
convert him into a true copy of a beast
who amputates contacts with the world
and primarily with his own self;
That's where the mirror plays the trick
manipulating his perceived image
into that of a chivalrous horseman
with the mindless logic of a fantasy,
the delusional trap of duex
turns personal and painfully tragic …

Not a bedtime story

These days I think
about making "choices",
What should my daughters see?
(whilst being acutely aware
there's nothing they cannot,
in the digital carnival of visuals!)
They're both in their teens
to them, a lot more world is unseen,
Could I share with them the tragedy
of being born as humans?
The gruesome scene
of one mammal killing another
is painful, toxic, traumatic,
perhaps leaving indelible scars
in their young, vibrant minds …
But, as a father
Should I not let them see the truth
of the state of the world?
To be sanguine in darkness
is to be misled by innocence,
leaving them more vulnerable
to the scheming predators;
But how could I tell them
that the world is not all about love
But a hell of hatred as well?
How could I torment their tender hearts

with the real stories of
deceptively human devilish shadows
await the opportunity to inflict violence?
How could I tear their hopes apart
by confessing that peace is a dream
and that as long as humans are here
The world would be in perpetual turmoil
In the battle between psyches?
Maybe, they should see the world as it is
in the clarity of light with vividness,
to titrate their expectations for humans
and to refine their fantastic dreams
through the sieve of reality;
It would no doubt make them sad
But it is infinitely better that they know
the unpredictable nature of humans,
The futility of having large craniums
That could well be a curse for humanity,
as overthinking kills the spirit of life,
and the eternal conflict of thoughts
would keep men at war forever …

The gallery of the undisplayable

Act 1
It was an urban place, where
people were standing in a beeline
with excitement in the air,
And above them hung a sign
"*Paris Garage*"!

The queue, winding and long,
displayed their sincere enthusiasm,
My hunch couldn't be wrong
though seen through a dreamy prism,
that it was an Art gallery!

I would be running late (I think)
better to be here on a quieter morning,
I catch a glimpse of a panel, my eyes blink
The painting is such a marvellous thing!
Sad I can't make it today

Act 2
I'm in a doctor's room, dimly lit
We talk about health-related things
Pointing to the wall, my eyes alight
I announce that those two are my drawings!
Pleased at heart is the patient!

The lady doctor consults a book
more of a guide than an imposing volume,
The "bloods "are strange, probably not mine
the wise man's belief (as per Hume)
is proportionate to the evidence!

It is noteworthy that the room is old
reminiscent of a clinic from younger days,
By then, that line of enquiry goes cold
and the cogent visuals part ways,
Every untold story is divided into chapters!

Act 3
The walkway is busy at the park
How surprised am I to see the politician
aged, infirm, draped in white like a stork!
But when he's unassuming like a plebeian
honestly I can't trust my eyes!

He is welcoming me to have free food
not just me, but every passer-by,
The vegetarian dishes do look good
But I craved for meat, to myself I cannot lie!
None more honest than a dreaming man!

It ought to be a sort of ritual feast
Maybe he's repenting for his life of sin!
But I admit I couldn't care the least
for a dream is not for moral warring …
Real hunger! as man is still alive in his dream

Act 4
I realise I'm close to the railway station
It's dark, the park around is deserted,
Closer to home! I'm on a vacation,
a long way away from where I had departed…
When night falls, people become moths!

It would soon be the break of dawn
As into thin air the art of the night vanishes
The dreamer continues his walk alone
ruminating over his unfulfilled wishes…
Back to reality, which is the beginning of another dream!…

Caution!

Do not
venture out into the bypaths
the clandestine alleyways
welcoming you with a grin
Like a spider casting its net
in the hard shell of the night!
"For you may get lost."

Remind yourself time and again
that you're still a child
and you'll always be one,
Do not look back at the lonely path
paved with the fallen shadows
of leaves and forgotten times
"*For you, maybe blinded by tears.*"

The angels lament from the pits
entangled in the web of memories,
Even the celestials aren't spared
from the trauma of the bygones;
The flowers are dead, the vase shattered
The shards are sharp like nails!
"*For memory is the congealed blood of life* "

The silence is intense and tormenting,
The ephemera cleared, light intervenes:

You can see things that are real,
reflecting the mouldy coffins of hopes;
Even the faintest note of music
maybe a respite from the visage of pain
"*For art is a retelling of memories.*"

The heart heaves, the eyes beseech
the bulwark of time to revert to a moment,
Then the realisation dawns of being mortal
helpless mammals stuck in the marshes,
fighting solely for their own survival,
soulless creatures with withered lives
"*For life is just the dream of a bee.*"

The lies are too many, the truth is singular
The shadows hasten down the paths
knowing they get nowhere;
Time is a closed loop; the web is intricate
But the insects are hopeful, for salvation,
as the demons within rest for a while
"*For there's nowhere to go, the trapdoor has closed!*"

Chrysalis on a crystal

You can't go in there!
Open is the door, real it seems
But it's forbidden, for the mortal
to be inside, the resident darkness
is welcoming though, bound to time
and unbreakable, but it isn't true
for a mural on a crystal, alluring
but innately fragile; the ochre
of earthly nostalgia, the blueness
of the skies unchanged! but (you know)
It doesn't last, the fragmented second
is all that is, the ephemeral cloud
transforms into figures, a subspecies
of humans exists in the dreams, let it be!
The genes, the blood, the cells are real
and they know you; the strangeness
of strangers is a fog, they're in the play
for the sake of the art, like the artist
painting Dorian Grey, the sitter becomes
the stimulus and passion; Dream is indeed
the reason of unreasonable, Wonderland
It is that which is burrowed into the rabbit
knows the labyrinth well, deceptive is
the looking glass, seductive, self-absorbed
selfishly holding onto the images, knowing
They don't last, yet the art blooms

creating streets out of alleyways, the corners
have talkative people, the vector of thoughts
transcending the space, another world
takes birth in parallel, undying but
impenetrable, as memory precipitates and
random clouds flock together, tunnelling
into the tunnel, an insane illusionist
throws away his illusions, the gist of life
births from ancient incantations, the child
doesn't heed and runs around, from one
to two to numberless holes, following
the shadow of the rabbit, only to lose
himself as the glass crumbles, the painting
ages against his best wishes, the imagery
dissipates into the mist, the walls come down
breaking the heart, the dream is over!…

The precipice

They say
Death is, after all, a prelude
to an extraordinary journey,
a sublimely beautiful one
that transcends time and space,
Though it would remain unknown
where the soul heads to,
the peaceful realm of the gods or
the dreadful circles of hell;
No more agonising breaths
the palpitations of the heart
the painful trials of earthly life
or ghosts of nightmarish fears,
The body without the mind
as the withered bark of wood
decays into natural elements,
devoid of the vitality of life,
sinking deeper into the womb
of the unheeding earth …
The empirical evidence of life
is the journey of life itself,
As for death is the stillness
frozen immobility of the corpse;
Whether there is a "world."
beyond the mind and intellect
in which every cell of the expired

inherits a purpose or meaning,
Whether in that sphere of invisibles
Life extends into the epilogue
with the trappings of divinity,
judgement amongst other things,
None can know whilst alive;
Perhaps, there's no point in knowing
The enigma of after-life
In which man doesn't exist anyway!
The soul that isn't human
that which knows no pain or sorrow
isn't even a vestige of the species,
as it has nothing to do with the body
or the precarious life it once lived;
The philosopher at the necropolis
has nothing to say to the world,
Whilst in life, he was brilliantly eloquent
and had the world listening
to every peak of wisdom from him,
Whether he was inducted into the netherworld
by the angelic winged commissionaire
Or all he met was the wave of darkness
and a blank page, nobody knows,
The tragedy of life is that
So much is unknown, even to the wise,
But there too lies the beauty of existence
In a perilous world, where time counts
and finitude looms large over the icons;
Being human is to deal with uncertainty
and to fight tooth and nail for survival,
But the poetic image of the butterfly

metamorphosing into a soul
is enamouring to the grief-stricken man,
who has to compel himself to believe
that amongst all the living beings
He alone is destined to be eternal …

Winter in the herbarium

If ever one could know
how the winter feels …
Shrouded in the white
of death, simple and pure,
the somber skies mourning
the loss of the leafy lives
who've left the earthly home,
The solitary bird at the apex
playing the descending melodies
of unequivocal sadness,
The absent signature of the sun
magnifying the loneliness
of the soul, perched on the seat
beside the emaciated fire,
The only respite is in the cup
of the caffeinated concoction
from the uncomplaining samovar …
The winds howl like a pack of wolves
seeking shelter in their motherly den,
The unhinged sleet is slithery,
The hazy walk is hazardous,
When the darkness is premature,
shadows play in the deserted park,
One needs to commit no crime
to be incarcerated by nature!
The inconspicuous greens on the trees

reminds one of the peril
That is inborn with life
Death indeed is a sibling of man,
impervious is the constant shadow …
The tattoos of grief on the walls
of the forgotten spring,
the lament of the sparrows
from the hollows in the woods,
The desolation of the homeless man
mirrored in his ever faithful dog,
the ancient tunes of melancholy
are embedded in the omniscient silence…
Man muses over the spiritual undertones
of the natural winter solstice,
Rekindling the fire of pregnant hopes
to reconcile with unassuaged grief,
He turns reclusive like the weather
to count the withered leaves
knowing that it is not worth knowing …
The dream creates a snowman
in the dilapidated backyard,
as fickle and enigmatic as snow,
Far away from the orphaned moors
A cry arises, that of a new human!
The joy of a long dark winter
enshrined in the warm red skin
of a new member of the species,
who has swam through the river of blood
to be mopped up by the towels
and put to the breasts of love!
Like a giant roaring laughter

It shatters the shackles of solitude,
The man regains his sanguine expression
as faint rays of morning light
dally along the sleepy meadows,
The snowman saunters like a child
dripping flakes all along the way
from the yard to the dark living room,
and kisses the half-awake man
with his cold carrot stick nose!...

The market of trifles

There's a *market*
for diseases making one sick
and medicines for all ilk,
There's a *market*
for works with paint and brush
after which enthusiasts would rush,
There's a *market*
for cinematically gift-wrapped love,
seeing which, lacrimal sacs overflow,
There's a *market*
for a hotchpotch of grief and loss
of the unfortunate with celebrity gloss,
There's a *market*
for the dreams of the downtrodden
and the unending pain of desolation,
There's a *market*
for the marrow of human suffering
The theme is often subjected to pilfering,
There's a *market*
for the plight of man in uncertainty
and for the criminal mind's notoriety,
There's a *market*
for the crimson ink of human blood
and the war-wrecked lives of the dead,
There's a *market*
for what hasn't been written as yet

and the tales of strangers in the gazette,
There's a *market*
for the boat that has capsized
and the corpses forensically sliced,
There's a *market*
for the outlier and the oddity
The thumb sticking out is a commodity!
There's a *market*
even in the mundane things
as long as the story is slightly insane,
The *market* thrives
feeding on the carcasses
of destroyed lives, and ones under duress,
The *market* revels
in its own acquired inhuman apathy
seeking sleaze in human agony,
The *market* has adapted
to ignore the pain of human existence
and to counter common sense,
The *market* knows
It's a demon in human disguise
to be a purveyor of sweetened lies!…

Plants in the old shoe

The past is dead
asserts Oscar Wilde!
No longer one of the tenants,
though his finer moments
remain, like dewed petals

of languid flower bells …
The ghost is a thought,
a hope painted in a white coat,
a feeling that time may not die
Though man knows it's a lie;
The memories are symbolically
images of wishful immortality,
They form the supportive cane
to walk through life; it isn't a bane
for a man to revisit the orphanage
of the abandoned bygone age,
to see his childhood in ruins
and feel the pained conscience;
Perhaps, that's how man survives
as he's an amalgam of many lives,
The child sleeps calmly within
as man tackles the maddening din,
The living man, too, has a ghost
a shadow of the times he has lost,
It serves as the loner's guide
the prism of pragmatism set aside,
the light of insight that stays vibrant
In an arrested life, lending a helping hand
for the aggrieved, desolate man to cope,
For him, only for him, time doesn't stop!
It isn't dead, the past is an illusion
The present is an anachronistic fusion,
The sentience of being alive in reality
is the key to the door of human duality,
He lives in the past alongside the present

under the endless illusionistic firmament,
If time indeed is dead, he too is dead
buried under the sprouts in the flowerbed …

Soulful Examination of Life

What seems to be the most evident
is the most evasive,
That's the irony of the self
that contradicts and confuses
the man piquant about his own life …

The self is the image of the mind
they say, without any solidity of proof,
Man is composed of thoughts like music,
The notes may not make sense per se
But the consummate experience is divine …

They lament about the spiritual soul
entrapped within the catacomb of a body,
Is the self a reflection of a living being?
Whilst the soul meditates on the other side,
One temporal, the other ethereal?…

The self could be the mirror within
that silently speaks the voice of conscience,
the radiance of which is like the sun
emits fiery energy in the realm of thoughts,
creating the existential duality of man…

To the world of people and myriad things
He belongs, and also to the world of his own
where the free spirit abounds in solitude,

The voice converses with him with ease,
Invisible are the vocal cords of the self …

How about the self of a demonic man
Who thrives in his unbridled monstrosity?
Precipitous is the track of human life,
a minefield of subjective interpretations;
Man is an animal that can justify himself being a beast!…

So the self of the devil ought to be devilish
Or is it unaffected by the selfish worldly life?
The sages sought the identification of the self with the soul
extrapolating the empirical world to the spiritual one,
The rock is tormented inside by the relentless waters …

Untouched by age and worldly temptations,
The subconscious is in a cosmic sleep,
What's breathing and conscious ought to be living
identifying with the elements of the natural world,
The other doesn't matter, it isn't made up of atoms …

The inward sight is painful but rewarding
The self is not beyond the natural order of things
but a collective abstraction of the elements,
The mirror that wouldn't break, and reflects
the passage to the soul and union with the universe …

Conflicted peace

A subconscious notion
is the dream, a concoction
of the happenings and imaginations,
It holds the essence of situations
with varied flavours of reality,
The incidents mixed with creativity
imbibing the hopes and fears
of the dreamer and his forebears …
The hands sketching the characters
of fiction reside in the quarters
of the human subconscious mind,
reminiscing about the tracks left behind
projecting the vitality of experience
to the future with prescience,
The evolutionary corpus of the collective
collaborating with the mind that's inventive
alchemising the elixir of deep hypnosis
that flies man to the lofts of the oasis,
where memories break the wall of silence
reading into every unread nuance
of the living experience, to deeply reflect
on the past for a surreal futuristic effect;
The conscious intervenes at a point
affecting the flow that's so fluent,
to barricade the lack of inhibitions
with patronising moralistic insinuations;

The segment of life spent in dreams
is not a haggard mind's fanciful whims,
but an intimate exploration of the self
In an attempt to bridge the gulf
between the worlds, real and imaginative
with illusions, seductive and deceptive,
as an antithesis to the reactive mindset,
reminding the pragmatic man not to forget
the indiscernible complexity of living life;
Dreaming gives meaning to the strife,
analyzing the shades of the actors
to see the flesh beneath the feathers;
For once, the conflicts seem inevitable
as life is deftly dramatised into a fable,
infused with the illusion of happenings
amidst a plethora of strange things,
with the heart seeking the islands
of hopes, whilst asleep on the moist sands
of reality like a dew drop on a rose petal
that at dawn has a story to tell ...

The unspoken

The mysterious skies do not speak
From the canopy, tears don't leak,
simply because it's an artwork
light applying its brilliant stroke
with no inclination to deceive,
What humans would perceive
is not the prerogative of nature,
The eyes are there to capture
the intricate anatomy of shapes,
But the mind seeks beyond the drapes
the exquisite pearls of the wisdom of life
to reassure itself that life's worth the strife,
The fourth wall barricades the sounds
as the restless mind does the rounds,
strenuously labouring to feel the music
that for mortal pain would be the analgesic;
The mind of man ventures to seek
the future, hoping for a sneak peek,
The musical score is subtle but poignant
As nature is silent like a meditating savant,
The skies of imagination are overcast
with doleful memories of the times lost,
In the mundane, man seeks the divine
knowing well his search would be in vain;
The fear chokes words from being uttered
But he clasps the straws of the most absurd

to reconcile with the reality of being alive
in the world, which is an insane beehive …

The cry

For fear of the devil
man trusts the benign god(s),
He knows evil is so banal
that he finds himself at odds
with his vision of destiny
that's deemed to be preordained;
But when he finds no sanctity
in the life that he has cleverly feigned,
The manipulator in him awakens
and gets busy with designing
the foundations of his moral tenets,
knowing well that he is simply lying
to himself, ashamed and dreadful
of his own image in the mirror
where he chances to face the ghoul
making him recoil with horror!...
He is such a strange mammal
who has lateral thoughts and insight
Yet his own soul he would sell
like a dark angel of the stormy night;
He is innately fearful of others,
the principal "other" being himself,
Hiding behind the plumage of feathers
Is the fabled blood lustful werewolf!
To banish the awareness of devilry
He weaves fanciful mythological tales,

He remains so insatiably power hungry
that his moral wagon often derails,
But he stubbornly believes in his own lies
unable to bear the blistering, glaring truth,
The woods resonate with his nocturnal cries
When in solitude, he would come to loathe
the insufferable abomination of his image
staring in deep from the broken glass,
Like a wild beast entrapped in a cage
He screams at the miserable icon of concealed flaws …

L'art de la survie

Art is not a vocation
It's not a weapon,
It's the essence of life
the truest sense of being…
    That which springs
    from the wells of the heart
    needs no medium of words
But even the endless restlessness
of the brush and the pen
wouldn't suffice to express in full
the pain of the tormented mind …
    Unanswerable are the "whys."
    the serpentine tracks of dreams
    the fragile cache of memories
    and the ephemera of space
    Torn apart between the worlds
    of a frivolous, frenzied life
    and the certitude of death,
    The fingers quiver with anguish
to voice the unvoiced
to break off from the mundane
like a meteoric piece of rock
dislodged from unending darkness
    to a dimensionless cosmos
    seeking the holy grail of freedom,
    absolute, pure, ineffable …